B... ^

MW01121469

my fell

MICHAEL

PLAYWRIGHTS

Low Creatures

RUBENFELD

CANADA PRESS

My Fellow Creatures © Copyright 2009 Michael Rubenfeld

PLAYWRIGHTS CANADA PRESS
The Canadian Drama Publisher
215 Spadina Ave., Suite 230, Toronto, Ontario, Canada, M5T 2C7
phone 416.703.0013   fax 416.408.3402
orders@playwrightscanada.com • www.playwrightscanada.com

For professional or amateur production rights, please contact Playwrights Canada Press at the address above.

The publisher acknowledges the support of the Canadian taxpayers through the Government of Canada Book Publishing Industry Development Program, the Canada Council for the Arts, the Ontario Arts Council, and the Ontario Media Development Corporation.

Cover and type design by Blake Sproule
Photography by Omer Yukseker
Interior photos depict Benjamin Clost as Kelly and Terrence Bryant as Arthur

LIBRARY AND ARCHIVES CANADA CATALOGUING IN PUBLICATION

Rubenfeld, Michael
My fellow creatures / Michael Rubenfeld.

A play.
ISBN 978-0-88754-861-1

I. Title.

PS8635.U29M94 2009   C812'.6   C2009-900105-5

First edition: January 2009
Printed and bound by Canadian Printco, Scarborough, Ontario, Canada

I've been asked a number of times why I decided to write on this topic. Why pedophilia?

At first I would have said that it was because I wanted to deal with the issue. I wanted to take it on. Explore it. Understand it. Help it breathe so that we can change it. Protect the children, etc., etc. Once I realized that I wasn't actually qualified to do any of these things, I was able to comfortably settle in to writing an incredibly complicated love story.

My Fellow Creatures presents an opportunity to explore the universal perplexity that is love in one of the most incomprehensible contexts imaginable.

There are those that would argue that this play has nothing to do with love and that pedophiles do not actually love children; that they are sick and twisted monsters.

But who are we to judge what is love and what is not?

Can anyone ever define what love is for another person?

Can anyone really define love?

This play is not a judgment of pedophiles. It is an exploration on the nature of love and relationship. Does it come to any conclusions?

I invite you to be its judge.

—Michael Rubenfeld
Toronto, 2008

My Fellow Creatures was first produced by Absit Omen Theatre in association with Buddies in Bad Times Theatre at Theatre Passe Muraille, Toronto, in May 2008.

The Cast was:

Arthur	Terrence Bryant
Kelly	Benjamin Clost
John	Richard Zeppieri

Directed by Michael Rubenfeld
Set & Costumes by Robin Fisher
Lighting by Kimberly Purtell
Original Music by Thomas Ryder Payne
Stage Managed by Joanna Barrotta
Dramaturgy by David Oiye
Production Associate – Alan Dilworth
Production Managed by Jonathan Rooke

*The original production was performed with the set in the middle of the theatre, surrounded on three sides by the audience.

My Fellow Creatures was originally developed through the Buddies In Bad Times Theatre Ante Chamber. It also received support through the Banff playRites Colony, Artscape's Gibraltor Point Residency Grant, Canada Council for the Arts, Ontario Arts Council, Toronto Arts Council and the Laidlaw Foundation.

Credit must be given to Don Hannah, Hannah Moscovitch, Meredith Vuchnich and Alan Dilworth for additional dramaturgical support.

No sympathy may I ever find. When I first sought it, it was the love of virtue, the feeling of happiness and affection with which my whole being overflowed, that I wished to be participated. But now, that virtue has become to me a shadow, and that happiness and affection are turned into bitter and loathing despair. . .

—Mary Shelley, *Frankenstein*

CHARACTERS

ARTHUR
KELLY
JOHN

SCENE ONE

Lights on a box. A small box. In the box is a toilet, a bed, a table. It's terrible. It's the worst box ever. No air. It's neat. Tidy. A radio sits on the table.

ARTHUR sits at his desk. There is food on the table. He writes in a journal. Music from the radio. Violins.

KELLY enters. He stands at the door. He stands there. Just stands. Watching. ARTHUR, sensing his presence, turns.

ARTHUR Excuse me?

KELLY exits.

Excuse me!

No response. ARTHUR contemplates going after him. He doesn't. He goes to his desk and to his writing. After a few moments KELLY reappears in the doorway. He stands there. Watching. ARTHUR turns off the radio.

KELLY doesn't move. They stare in silence. Something familiar.

KELLY still says nothing.

Who are you?

Still no response.

Darling, I asked you a question.

Beat.

ARTHUR moves slightly forward. KELLY moves slightly back.

I don't bite.

ARTHUR goes back to his desk. He sits. He takes his food and begins to eat.

KELLY re-enters. We barely see him lingering near the cell. ARTHUR spots him and stops eating. He turns back towards KELLY.

Do you find it dark in here?

I think a larger window would be nice.

Beat.

Do you like windows?

Beat.

Do you like light?

Beat.

It's unnerving. Unnatural. To live in darkness.

And yet, somehow so familiar. Something so… honest. Mysterious.

ARTHUR picks up a piece of meat from his plate.

What do you think that is?

ARTHUR takes a bite. Chews.

Tastes like…

He takes another bite.

Let's call it veal, shall we?

Beat.

Veal. Hm. Veal. Veal. Veal. Veal. There's something so inhumane about ripping young calves from their mother's breast.

ARTHUR takes another bite.

Arthur.

3

My name. Like the king.

KELLY stops eating.

My name, is Arthur.

KELLY   …

ARTHUR   This is the part where you tell me your name.

Beat.

Is it… Alexander?

Gregory?

I give up.

Beat.

You look like a Christian. Is it Christian?

I've always been fond of Christians. Real Christians. Envious, really.

They have such a… bond between life and love. He was a noble leader. Christ. Dreadful carpenter… so I hear.

ARTHUR takes another bite.

Do you believe in God?

Beat.

Too personal?

Still nothing.

Do you have faith?

Beat.

It's a difficult thing to hold onto here. Faith. If you have it I encourage you to—

KELLY exits.

. . .

He's gone. ARTHUR continues to eat in silence.

Lights.

SCENE TWO

Lights. Evening. ARTHUR stands outside his cell. JOHN, a C.O. (guard) is inspecting the cell.

He strips the bed.

ARTHUR   I just made that.

JOHN continues to search.

I hate this part.

JOHN   It's my job.

JOHN finishes up.

Clean.

ARTHUR   It's always clean.

JOHN moves to the desk. He begins searching.

ARTHUR enters the cell and starts to remake his bed.

JOHN   What are you doing?

ARTHUR   What?

JOHN   What do you think you're doing?

ARTHUR   I'm making the—

JOHN   Out.

ARTHUR looks at him surprisingly.

JOHN   OUT.

ARTHUR exits the cell.

JOHN goes back to the desk.

JOHN   The prisoner must remain outside the cell until the inspection is complete.

Those are the rules.

ARTHUR   You're an excellent guard, John.

JOHN   You know the rules.

ARTHUR   Honestly. An inspiration.

JOHN finishes his search.

7

JOHN   Clean. You can come in now.

> *ARTHUR re-enters and starts to make the bed.*

Is this going to be a problem in the future?

ARTHUR   No.

JOHN   Are you sure?

ARTHUR   Yes.

JOHN   Will you need a reminder?

ARTHUR   No.

JOHN   Will you need anything?

ARTHUR   Parole.

> *Beat.*

That was a joke.

JOHN   You could have it.

ARTHUR   But the rent here is so reasonable—and the guards are so skilled.

> *JOHN goes to exit.*

The new one. Who is he?

JOHN   Kelly?

ARTHUR   Yes. Kelly.

JOHN   Why you asking?

ARTHUR   He's very quiet.

JOHN   So were you.

ARTHUR   Was I?

JOHN   According to your file.

ARTHUR   You've read my file?

JOHN   I read everyone's file.

ARTHUR   Impressive.

JOHN   It's my job.

ARTHUR   So I've heard.

        KELLY comes to the cell. They see him.

JOHN   *(to KELLY)* What?

        KELLY goes to leave.

ARTHUR   Stay, Kelly.

        KELLY's surprised that he knows his name. Pause.

Thank you John.

JOHN   For what?

ARTHUR   Your inspection.

JOHN   Oh. Right. Yeah, well, everything looks fine. So… don't…

> *Beat.*

All right?

> *JOHN looks at KELLY.*

What?

> *JOHN goes to leave. KELLY's blocking the path.*

You're in my way.

> *KELLY moves out of the way.*

Don't get in my way. Okay?

> *JOHN exits. KELLY doesn't move.*

ARTHUR   Are you coming in?

> *KELLY enters the cell, taking out a cigarette.*

Please don't smoke in my home.

This is where I live. This is my home.

10

KELLY   I smoke everywhere else.

ARTHUR   This is not "everywhere else."

> *KELLY puts the cigarette behind his ear. He looks off into the distance. ARTHUR sits and watches him, waiting for him to do something. Anything.*

Shall we walk?

In the yard.

KELLY   Why?

ARTHUR   Because it would be nice.

KELLY   Nice?

ARTHUR   Nice.

> *Beat.*

KELLY   Why should you get nice?

ARTHUR   Everyone deserves a little "nice."

KELLY   You don't.

> *Beat.*

ARTHUR   I.... Oh?

I see.

You...

Hm.

Beat.

This may be difficult for you to understand, but in this wing, people like... myself... are free to... live harmoniously. We come and go as we please. We have the freedom to do nice things like walk in the yard.

We are free to accept visitors. Guests.

But there are rules in this wing.

You're not allowed to judge me in this wing. Understand?

KELLY snickers. ARTHUR works to restrain himself.

Do you know me? Do you know what goes on in my head? In my heart?

ARTHUR's getting upset.

Please leave.

KELLY doesn't move.

Out. Out of my cell.

Still he doesn't leave.

GET OUT!

KELLY goes to the toilet and pukes.

ARTHUR slowly moves to KELLY. He puts his hand on his back.

Child?

KELLY flinches. ARTHUR moves back.

KELLY goes to exit.

Rest.

KELLY exits. ARTHUR walks out after him. JOHN lingers.

JOHN   What was that about?

Beat.

Arthur!

ARTHUR   He was angry with me. For why I'm here. Who I am.

JOHN   Who you are?

Did you ask him who he is?

He's a hound. Like you.

A revelation. A surprise.

JOHN exits. Lights.

13

SCENE THREE

> *Lights. The cell is empty. Then, quickly, KELLY walks past the cell.*

ARTHUR *(offstage)* Kelly!

> *ARTHUR appears on stage.*

Stop!

KELLY You've been here twelve years—you should be out by now.

ARTHUR Who have you been talking to?

KELLY Everyone knows. You're famous.

ARTHUR You flatter me.

KELLY Pig.

ARTHUR Am I? And what's your excuse?

KELLY goes to exit.

I know why you're here. You're just like me.

KELLY   I'm not.

ARTHUR   Talk to me, Kelly, tell me why you're like me.

KELLY   I'm not like you. I know what I did was wrong.

ARTHUR   According to whom?

KELLY   EVERYONE.

ARTHUR   Everyone. Always there, isn't he. Poking his nose into other people's business. Who is everyone, Kelly? Most of the men in this wing are lovers of children—they have relations with young children—here, they are the majority—here, they are everyone. Is that who you speak of?

KELLY   The people here are sick.

ARTHUR   According to whom? If we were the only two people in the world we would be everyone—you and I. Would we still be wrong?

KELLY   Yes.

ARTHUR   But everyone in the world says we're not wrong. How could we be wrong? Your argument is lacking.

KELLY   I don't care.

ARTHUR You aren't the most skilled communicator, are you.

KELLY Maybe I don't want to communicate with you.

ARTHUR Take responsibility for your actions. Don't look to "everyone." Look to yourself.

KELLY exits quickly.

JOHN enters.

Always keeping an eye on me, aren't you?

JOHN It's my job.

JOHN enters.

Want to tell me what that was about?

ARTHUR He's needs help.

JOHN He's in a program.

ARTHUR Everyone's in a "program."

JOHN They help a lot of people.

ARTHUR With what? Fixing them?

Do you think I need to be fixed, John?

JOHN I think you need to watch your step.

Beat.

ARTHUR   He's alone. He's confused.

JOHN   Those are the consequences.

ARTHUR   For what? Love?

JOHN   For breaking the law, Arthur. He broke the law.

ARTHUR   What would you do if you were condemned for your love? If you were told you were wrong to feel pure, honest, love? If you were forced to suffer through heartbreak, day in day out, no reprieve, no understanding, nothing but bars, cement and a good guard to keep you company.

JOHN   I'd take a program. I'd get some help. I'd try to get over it and move on.

ARTHUR   Move on...

JOHN   That's right.

ARTHUR   Just like that?

JOHN   That's right.

ARTHUR   You really are an excellent guard. Your ability to put your job before all is quite extraordinary.

JOHN goes to exit.

I see you too have moved on.

JOHN stops.

Your wedding ring.

JOHN   What about it?

ARTHUR   It's gone.

JOHN   So?

ARTHUR   I just assumed—

JOHN   You assumed what?

ARTHUR   I'm sorry, it's really none of my business.

JOHN   No, it really isn't.

JOHN exits. He then returns.

And for the record, we're just taking some time apart, all right, it's no big deal. So don't go making assumptions.

ARTHUR   My apologies. It won't happen again. I pinky swear.

JOHN exits.

ARTHUR turns on the radio.
Lights fade.

He exits.

SCENE FOUR

Lights. Next evening. KELLY alone in ARTHUR's cell. ARTHUR's in the yard. He is looking very quickly through ARTHUR's things. He looks behind him periodically. JOHN walks by. He sees KELLY. He doesn't do anything. He stands, watching. KELLY doesn't notice him. KELLY looks through some of ARTHUR's books. He can't find it.

KELLY turns and sees JOHN.

No one says anything. This is not good.

JOHN enters the cell.

JOHN   Sit.

KELLY does. JOHN sits and stares at him.

We haven't formally met.

KELLY   I wasn't—

JOHN   Ssssshhhhhhh.

            Beat.

            Kelly, right?

            I'm John. My friends call me John.

            When I was younger people called me Johnny, or
            sometimes they called me an asshole. But I'm not an
            asshole, Kelly. I'm actually a very nice person.

            Beat.

            How's it going for you in here? How are you
            adjusting?

            Beat.

            Rule number one: when a superior asks you a question,
            you answer.

KELLY   It's fine.

JOHN   You're adjusting fine?

KELLY   Yes.

JOHN   Oh yeah? That's good. That's very good.

            Beat.

            How's your program?

KELLY   Good.

JOHN   What's good about it?

         Beat.

         What's good about it?

KELLY   I don't know.

JOHN   Why don't you know?

         Beat.

         Why don't you know?

KELLY   Because I don't—I don't know, I don't know what you
         want me to say.

JOHN   Hey, now just take it easy. No need to get worked up.

         Beat.

         This is a nice cell, don't you think?

KELLY   …Yeah.

JOHN   If I were living here I think I'd want to live in a cell like
         this.

         I like the window. This is a nice desk. Pretty fancy
         radio. Do you have a radio?

KELLY   No.

JOHN   Would you like a radio?

KELLY   Sure.

JOHN   I wasn't offering. It was only a question.

I'm a guard. It's my job to get to know the people I'm guarding.

Now, you're in a prisoner's cell without their permission. Some people call that bad behaviour. Some people call that "breaking and entering." I call that fucking up. Is that what you want to be?

A fuck-up?

Beat.

You ever read *Frankenstein*?

KELLY shakes his head.

Bet you seen the movie though, huh?

KELLY   Yes.

JOHN   Nothing like the book.

KELLY   No?

JOHN   Totally different. In the movie the monster's played like a total idiot. Really stupid. He's not like that in the book. In the book the monster's smart. Really smart. In the movie he's just a crazy monster who kills people. They never actually explain why he's killing people.

Beat.

Why do you think the monster killed people?

KELLY   Because he's a monster?

JOHN   No! It's because he didn't have anyone to care about him. That's all he wanted. Somebody to care about him. Somebody to help him not be a fuck-up.

Beat.

What do you think about that?

KELLY   What do you think?

JOHN   I think the monster got a bad rap in the movie.

Beat.

I know what you're thinking. You're thinking, "Why's he talking to me about *Frankenstein*?" I'll tell you why. I think that you're not much different than the monster. The book monster. But everyone else thinks you're the movie monster. I think you got yourself a bad rap, and I imagine it must be really difficult for you to be in here. I imagine you're really confused, 'cause all you want is someone to care about you. Does that sound right?

KELLY   Sure.

JOHN   I know why you're here. What you did.

         I know a lot of people like you. I make it my job to be
         generous to people like you, even when no one else is.
         Even though I got two little girls at home.

KELLY   Good thing I only like little boys.

         Beat.

JOHN   You think that's funny?

KELLY   No.

JOHN   That's not funny.

KELLY   I know.

         Beat.

JOHN   Nobody likes a fuck-up, Kelly. You can choose to be a
         fuck-up or you can choose to not be a fuck-up.

         Beat.

         What's it gonna be?

         JOHN smiles.

         Don't be a fuck-up. Okay?

Okay?

KELLY   Okay.

JOHN   Okay?

Okay.

I'm glad we talked. That was a really good talk, don't you think? I feel like we're closer now. Do you feel like we're closer?

KELLY   …Yeah.

JOHN   Good. It's important to be close to people.

Thank you… for the talk.

> *Beat.*

You should read that book. *Frankenstein.* You might learn something.

KELLY   Okay.

JOHN   You promise?

KELLY   I pinky swear. Can I go now?

JOHN   Free country.

> *JOHN laughs.*

KELLY exits.

JOHN looks around. Opens a drawer. ARTHUR enters, JOHN doesn't see him.

ARTHUR   Anything of interest?

JOHN closes the drawer, startled.

JOHN   I wasn't...

No. Everything looks fine.

ARTHUR   Was I scheduled for another inspection?

JOHN   No.

ARTHUR   I see.

Courtesy call?

JOHN   Something like that.

Beat.

ARTHUR   Are you staying for dinner?

JOHN   No, I gotta... oh. That was a joke.

That's funny.

ARTHUR   Ha ha ha.

Beat.

JOHN   Yeah, well, everything's in order here.

ARTHUR   Such diligence.

JOHN   It's my job.

ARTHUR   Good guarding.

    JOHN goes to exit.

And the wife?

JOHN   What about her?

ARTHUR   Everything in order there?

    Beat.

JOHN   Not yet.

    Beat.

ARTHUR   And have you told her how you feel?

JOHN   About what?

ARTHUR   About how you feel.

JOHN   I don't know how I feel.

ARTHUR   I see. How do you think you feel?

JOHN exits.

ARTHUR goes to the drawer. He opens it and looks inside. He looks behind him. Nobody. He goes to the radio. He opens it from the bottom and quickly checks to see that the letters are still there.

He goes into the drawer and takes out a book. The Once and Future King. *He exits.*

Lights.

SCENE FIVE

Lights.

The cell is empty.

KELLY walks by. He stops, sees that the cell is empty. He looks in, contemplates going. He looks around. No one is there. He looks into the cell again. ARTHUR enters. He sees KELLY looking into the cell. KELLY sees ARTHUR and goes to exit.

ARTHUR   Hi.

KELLY stops.

Are we okay?

He walks past KELLY and into his cell. He sits. KELLY stands at the cell.

Pause.

29

Have you been outside? Gorgeous! Not a cloud for miles.

Beat.

Do you like reading? I find it passes the time.

Beat.

What's your sentence?

KELLY   Four.

ARTHUR   You must be in a program.

    KELLY nods his head.

How's that working out? Does it help?

KELLY   They tell me I'm sick.

ARTHUR   Well that's not very nice, is it?

    Beat.

Did you use force?

KELLY   No.

ARTHUR   Did you make him do anything he didn't want to?

KELLY   He was eleven.

ARTHUR   Did he love you?

Did he tell you he loved you?

Beat.

Did he?

KELLY   Yes.

ARTHUR   Did you love him?

Beat.

Did you tell him you loved him?

KELLY   Yes.

ARTHUR   And did you believe that? When you looked at him. When you touched him. Did you believe, with all your heart, that you loved that child?

Beat.

I did.

I loved him.

He gave me love that I've never felt before. He wrote me letters. He was poetic. Ten years old. How many children are poetic?

They have so much love, Kelly. Did you not feel that? That trust? That unconditional love? That clarity.

31

To be trusted so fully. To give my love so fully.

To be sought after. To be touched. To be explored.

Such magical curiosity. Don't you see? We can't argue with the instincts of a child. We shouldn't.

Beat.

What we've done we did for the right reasons. You have to believe that. It's all we have. Our integrity. Our love. You acted according to your true, sincere feelings for another individual, and it's beautiful.

KELLY stands. Stares. Amazed.

What is it? What?

KELLY almost says something, but instead leaves.

He's gone.

JOHN enters.

JOHN   The doctors are having a hard time getting through to him.

ARTHUR   So am I.

JOHN   In three years—less—he'll be eligible for parole. He'll be able to start over. Have a new life.

ARTHUR   And then what? He'll live happily ever after? You think

32

he's going to change?

JOHN   With the proper help.

ARTHUR   Oh, right. Help. Free at last.

JOHN   Not everyone thinks like you.

ARTHUR   Not everyone thinks.

Beat.

JOHN   Most people want to get out of here as soon as they can, but you, no, not you, you'd rather, what, you'd rather—you'd rather—what?! What are you trying to prove? Do you want to die in here?

         Just take the program. Get your parole. Get out of here. Go swimming. It's fun!

Beat.

ARTHUR   Swimming.

Beat.

         John, out there I can only be who they tell me I am. In here.... This is who I am, John. This is me.

Beat.

         And you? Who are you?

33

JOHN   Your guard.

ARTHUR   Are you? What does your wife say?

JOHN   About what?

ARTHUR   Who you are.

Beat.

JOHN   She says she doesn't know who I am.

ARTHUR   How does it make you feel?

JOHN   Like a bowl of fucking cherries.

Beat.

ARTHUR   And have you considered leaving this place?

JOHN   And do what?

ARTHUR   Go swimming.

Beat.

JOHN   That kid you're trying to help? He was in here. The other day.

Beat.

ARTHUR   Go on.

JOHN   That's it. I found him in here looking around.

ARTHUR   What kind of looking?

JOHN   Just looking. Do you want to press charges?

ARTHUR   No. But thank you.

You're a good guard, John.

A good man, also.

JOHN   Tell that to my wife.

ARTHUR   In a heartbeat.

Beat.

JOHN turns and heads towards the door.

JOHN   LIGHTS OUT!

JOHN exits.

Lights.

SCENE SIX

Lights.

ARTHUR, alone in his cell. Music. ARTHUR is writing.

KELLY comes to the door. He enters the cell. He stands behind ARTHUR. ARTHUR knows he's there. ARTHUR puts his journal away and turns towards KELLY. They are inches from each other.

ARTHUR What do you want?

What do you want, Kelly?

Beat.

Do you want my help? Do you want me to help you, Kelly?

What do you want?

What were you looking for? The other day. In my cell.

What do you want.

What do you want?

What do you want?

What do you want?

KELLY   I DON'T KNOW WHAT I WANT. WHAT DO YOU WANT? WHAT DO YOU WANT FROM ME!? You want to help? Stop talking. For one second. All you do is talk and talk and talk and talk and talk. I feel like punching you in the face.

ARTHUR   So punch me.

KELLY punches him.

KELLY   When I think about what I've done... when I think about how much damage I've caused. I think about that child, his life—how nothing will make sense for him anymore.

The things we did. How could I? How could you?

ARTHUR   This is who we are, Kelly. Our love is not a choice, it is who we are. There are hundreds and thousands of us. We've always been here and we'll always be here whether everyone likes it or not.

KELLY goes to exit.

If you were still together.... If you'd not been caught—

KELLY   I wasn't caught. I turned myself in.

He, again, tries to exit.

ARTHUR   Wait!

ARTHUR goes to the radio. He takes out the letters. He brings them to KELLY and offers them to him.

These are letters that he wrote to me. A testament of his love. Read them. You'll see what our love was like.

KELLY exits.

Keep them safe. Don't let anyone see you with them.

JOHN appears.

JOHN   What do you want from him?

ARTHUR   The same thing you want, John. To protect him.

JOHN   That's my job—It is my JOB to protect the inmates / of this—

ARTHUR   How can you protect your inmates when you can't protect your own family?

Pause.

That was unfair. I regret saying that.

Beat.

John?

JOHN   No, y'know what, no, you're right.

ARTHUR   I'm not.

JOHN   No, you're right. You're right.

> *Beat.*

What the hell do I know, right? I'm just a fucking guard, what do I know? I mean, what the fuck am I doing here anyways, right?

> *JOHN laughs.*

Hey, get this. My wife wants to leave me. She says I'm fucking crazy, working in a place like this, taking care of people like you. She says I'm losing perspective.

Do you think I'm losing perspective?

ARTHUR   Do you?

JOHN   No. But that's just my perspective.

39

Says she doesn't know how I can work in a place like this and then come and kiss our kids good night.

You have sex with children. That's what she said. She said, "They have sex with children, that means they're sick."

And that's the thing, right, that's where she's got a pretty good point, 'cause that's the thing that I don't understand either. How can you have sex with a kid?

Beat.

Arthur?

ARTHUR   You can't choose your love, John.

JOHN   But you can choose who you fuck.

Beat.

ARTHUR   Love is not a choice, John.

Beat.

JOHN   Maybe I am losing perspective.

Pause.

ARTHUR   I'm sorry for your difficulties with your family.

Beat.

ARTHUR lingers for a second and then exits.

JOHN also goes to exit.

KELLY enters quickly, letters in hands. He sees JOHN and hides the letters.

KELLY   Where is he?

Beat.

He was just here.

JOHN   He left.

KELLY doesn't move.

What do you want?!

Beat.

WHAT?

Beat.

KELLY   What would you do if I did something to one of your daughters?

Beat.

JOHN   I'd rip your fucking head off.

JOHN moves quickly towards KELLY.

KELLY   Y'know in two years I'm eligible for parole. There's no telling what I could do.

> *KELLY smiles/snickers. JOHN punches KELLY in the stomach.*

> *KELLY lies on the ground.*

> *ARTHUR returns. He has juice in his hands. He takes in the sight.*

ARTHUR *(to JOHN)* Juice?

> *He offers juice to JOHN.*

> *JOHN takes it. He opens it and he drinks.*

> *He exits.*

> *KELLY removes the letters from his pocket and reads.*

KELLY "I love you, Arthur. I love how you make me feel. I love how you take care of me. I love how you love me."

ARTHUR I did love him.

KELLY I know. I know you did.

Daniel. That's a nice name.

ARTHUR He was so beautiful.

> *Beat.*

He would walk through the door and it was as if the world had stopped except for him. This beautiful, perfect boy. I would have done anything for him.

KELLY   Would you have stopped if he had asked you to?

ARTHUR   Of course. We could have stopped at any time.

I told him that most people would choose to not understand our love.

KELLY   Did he understand why?

ARTHUR   He did. It was his idea to keep it a secret.

KELLY   And look at you now.

ARTHUR   That's right. Look. Here I sit. Alone in my box. Away from the world. Away from my love.

He loved me so much.

Beat.

What's his name?

Beat.

Your love.

KELLY   …Andy.

ARTHUR   Do you miss him?

43

KELLY   Sometimes.

ARTHUR   What do you miss about him?

Beat.

KELLY   His youth.

Beat.

ARTHUR   Why did you turn yourself in?

KELLY   …

ARTHUR   Did he want you to leave him?

KELLY   He didn't know what he wanted.

ARTHUR   He's probably thinking about you right now.

KELLY   He probably is.

He's probably feeling very upset, crying, as a doctor tries to explain to him how wrong our behaviour was. He's probably sitting in a corner of his bedroom feeling guilty and alone and afraid and confused and wondering why I'm gone, why I left.

He didn't know. He didn't know and I knew that and I didn't care. He said I love you. He said thank you. He hugged me. He touched me. He did what I wanted him to do, and that's why he did it. Because I wanted him to. He wanted to make me happy—as happy as I made him.

ARTHUR   And what's wrong with that?

          It's what you both wanted.

KELLY   He's a child.

ARTHUR   He loves you.

KELLY   What does a ten-year-old know about love?

ARTHUR   Everything.

KELLY   I took advantage of him.

ARTHUR   You loved him.

KELLY   It was wrong. I knew it was wrong.

ARTHUR   Then why did you? If you were so clear about how
          wrong you were—why did you? Why do it at all?

KELLY   Because I'm sick.

ARTHUR   Take some responsibility.

          You loved that boy—and you loved his body.

          You can tell me you're sick all you want, but that's the
          facts. Are you going to just "get better"? Are you going
          to change that about you?

          You think your program is going to change that?

45

We're human beings, Kelly. We're not robots. We can't just be rewired.

You want to be sick? Fine. Be sick. I'm going to be "not sick." I may die in here, but at least I'll have lived my life honestly.

KELLY And what about Daniel!?

How is he supposed to live his life? Now that you're here, living your "honest" life... now that you've ruined his life—what's HE supposed to do?

ARTHUR Is that what you think?

KELLY It's not what I think. It's what I know.

Look at me, Arthur.

LOOK AT ME.

LOOK AT ME!!

Are you that blind?

Do you really not see?

You want to know what I was doing in your cell?

THESE. I was looking for these.

To see if you kept them.

These letters I wrote to you.

These fucking letters that haunt me.

This fucking life!

Have I grown up that much?

Do you really not see?

Or maybe you just don't want to.

Twelve years, Arthur.

That's right.

Take a good look. Look at this. Look at me.

    Beat.

ARTHUR Daniel.

    Beat.

My God.

Impossible.

KELLY   Believe what you want to believe. I don't give a shit what you believe.

    KELLY exits. ARTHUR sits. Stunned. Black.

SCENE SEVEN

Lights.

ARTHUR lies in his bed. Music plays. He's in a sort of haze.

He gets up from his bed. He goes to the radio. He turns it off. He opens the radio and he takes out the letters. He stares at them for a second.

And then. . . he drops the radio onto the ground.

JOHN enters.

He sees the radio.

ARTHUR I thought I'd redecorate.

Nice, isn't it?

I like the subtleness of the black against the grey.

JOHN   Arthur...

ARTHUR   Oh, hello, John, didn't see you there. Did you get a haircut?

JOHN   Arthur!

ARTHUR   You look quite dapper.

JOHN   Pick up the radio.

ARTHUR   Radio? What radio?

JOHN   On the floor.

ARTHUR   Oh look! A radio! Hello, radio. Hello. Hello!

         ARTHUR playfully kicks his chair over. It lands on the ground.

         That looks quite fetching.

         Do you think we could take out that back wall?

         There's something different about you—is that—have you been working out?

JOHN   You're out of line.

ARTHUR   So punish me. I'm out of line, John. Put me back in line.

         ARTHUR laughs.

JOHN   Stop it.

ARTHUR continues to laugh.

ARTHUR!

ARTHUR   John!

JOHN   STOP IT!

ARTHUR   Jooohhhnnn!

JOHN   Pick up the chair.

ARTHUR   John.

JOHN   Now!

ARTHUR   Johnny?

JOHN   NOW!

JOHN shoves ARTHUR to the ground.

ARTHUR picks up the chair. He sits in it.

What's wrong with you?

ARTHUR   …

JOHN   Answer me.

Beat.

Arthur, I asked you a question.

ARTHUR I'm sorry, what was the question?

JOHN What the fuck's wrong with you?

ARTHUR sings Patsy Cline's "Crazy."

JOHN Do you want time in the hole?

ARTHUR Yes.

JOHN You do?

ARTHUR Yes.

JOHN Stop fucking around.

ARTHUR No.

JOHN Arthur!

ARTHUR Shhhh. Shhh, John. Look at you. So angry. This is no place for you.

JOHN I don't know what you're doing or what you think—

ARTHUR You need to leave now.

JOHN What?

ARTHUR Leave me alone.

Pause.

JOHN exits.

ARTHUR picks the radio up from the ground. He begins to dance with it while continuing to sing.

JOHN returns, aggressively bringing KELLY into the cell.

Get him out of here.

JOHN   No, we're going settle this RIGHT NOW.

ARTHUR   I don't want him here.

JOHN   I don't care!

Beat.

Somebody tell me what the fuck is going on here!

Beat.

Answer the question!

KELLY   What was the question?

JOHN   You know the question.

KELLY   Refresh my memory.

JOHN   What is going on?

Beat.

KELLY   Arthur? Do you want to take this one?

Beat.

We fuck children, John.

ARTHUR   Don't be crass.

JOHN   Fuck you.

ARTHUR   *(to JOHN)* He just wants to hurt people.

KELLY   Like the way you hurt Daniel?

JOHN   Who's Daniel?

KELLY   You don't know?

JOHN   No, I don't fucking know—who's Daniel?

KELLY   Daniel was a ten-year-old boy who trusted his psychiatrist. His dad died and his mom was too upset to deal with it, so he turned to Arthur for help. And then Arthur took advantage of him. He made him believe that some things were okay, but those things weren't okay.

ARTHUR   I didn't make him do—

KELLY   I didn't know what I was doing.

ARTHUR   You know you did!

KELLY   Ten years old!

ARTHUR   You made your own decisions.

KELLY   I did what you wanted me to do.

JOHN   Everybody SLOW DOWN.

> *Beat.*

> (*to KELLY*) Are you Daniel?

> *Nobody says anything.*

Are you Daniel!?

> *KELLY laughs.*

ARTHUR   John, go.

JOHN   What?

ARTHUR   Please, John.

JOHN   I'm in charge here.

ARTHUR   John. Please. Listen to me.

JOHN   (*to KELLY*) Shut up!

ARTHUR   This is not your responsibility.

JOHN   I'm trying to help. *(to KELLY)* Shut up!

ARTHUR   Please. John. I need you to trust me.

             KELLY laughs.

             John, GO!

             JOHN goes to KELLY and punches him and pushes him to the ground.

JOHN   I SAID SHUT UP! SHUT UP! SHUT UP!

             Pause.

             Arthur, tell me what's going on.

             What's going on?

             What's going on, Arthur.

             Arthur? What's going on?

             Arthur?

             ARTHUR.

             ARTHUR!

ARTHUR   You can't fix this, John. We're different than you. This has nothing to do with you.

             Look at what's happening. This isn't what you want.

55

Beat.

John...

Call your wife.

Leave.

Leave.

> *JOHN looks at KELLY. He looks back at ARTHUR.*

JOHN   Arthur...?

ARTHUR   It's okay.

It's okay.

> *JOHN exits.*
>
> *Pause.*
>
> *KELLY laughs.*

Why didn't you say anything?

KELLY   Why didn't you recognize me?

> *Beat.*

ARTHUR   What do you want from me?

KELLY   Do you think I LIKE seeing you?

ARTHUR   Do you want to see me punished? / Is that it?

KELLY   You deserve it.

ARTHUR   Did you even love that child?

KELLY   I loved you.

ARTHUR   What do you want from me?

KELLY   Look at what you've made me. / Look at me.

ARTHUR   I can't believe you knew / this entire time.

KELLY   You were my teacher.

ARTHUR   I've been trying to help you.

KELLY   When have you helped me?

ARTHUR   All I've ever done is try to help you.

KELLY   How? By leaving me?

> *Beat.*

Why did you leave me?

ARTHUR   I was arrested.

KELLY   Why did you do this to me?

ARTHUR   It wasn't a choice.

KELLY   Do you know how many men I've fucked just because they looked like you? Do you know what a hell my life has been since you left? Do you know what they do to kids like me?

They told me it was wrong. They told me everything we did, all our time together—they told me it was wrong.

Why didn't you tell me it was wrong?

They told me you were bad—that I'd never see you again and that I was safe. I didn't feel safe. My mother couldn't even look at me. She kept saying things like "What happened to you?" and "What's wrong with you?"

I changed my name. I tried to start over.

How do I start over? How do I get better?

ARTHUR takes the letters.

ARTHUR   These. For twelve years I've kept these.

He goes into his drawer and takes out books of writing.

Look. These. All for you. I've written to you. For twelve years I've been writing letters to you. The way we used to. Remember? They're all here, you can read them—they're yours.

All this is for you. I did this for you. This is why I'm here. This is what's kept me alive. You. It's always been you. Everything I am. Every ounce of my being has been for you.

Beat.

It's okay. I'm right here, Kelly.

You're okay.

KELLY   I'm not.

ARTHUR   You are. I'm telling you that you are.

ARTHUR moves towards KELLY.

KELLY   Don't.

Beat. ARTHUR makes another move towards him.

Stay away.

ARTHUR puts his arms around him. He holds him. KELLY allows it for a moment and then pushes ARTHUR away.

You smell awful. You need a shower.

ARTHUR   I do. I need a shower.

KELLY   You never used to smell like that.

Beat.

Why? Why did you love me?

Why did you have to love me?

Beat.

Please tell me.

ARTHUR You were so perfect. So gentle.

Beat.

You were such a curious child.

KELLY All children are curious.

ARTHUR Not like you. The way you experienced the world was extraordinary. So rare. We'd have the most wonderful, honest conversations about art, love, life—you would tell me things. About your mother. About her struggles after your father died. You would talk of your concern for her. Your love for her was so...

Questions! You'd ask the most wonderful questions.

I never had to work to be around you. The ease of your company. The way you laughed at my jokes.

KELLY I remember laughing a lot.

ARTHUR All the time.

You made me feel like a child.

Do you know how special that is?

KELLY   It was special, wasn't it? I've always thought that.

ARTHUR   Yes… yes.

> *Beat.*

KELLY   And then what happened?

ARTHUR   And then…?

And then… we fell in love.

It was never planned. I didn't understand it. But it happened.

I loved you. I'd never truly allowed myself to love until you.

> *Beat.*

Do you remember how we would wrestle?

KELLY   You would let me win.

ARTHUR   I loved letting you win.

KELLY   I loved winning.

> *Beat.*

I was a really nice boy.

> *Beat.*

61

I remember what you smelled like.

I remember your cologne. Do you remember that?

Do you remember what I smelled like?

Did I smell good?

ARTHUR   Yes.

KELLY   That's good.

That's good.

I remember how you would lean over and you would put your nose on my neck and you would smell me and make a little noise.

I always liked that. I still dream of that.

Beat.

I don't think I smell good anymore.

After you were gone that's the thing I kept thinking all the time. How bad I must smell now.

I actually thought that maybe that's why you left. Because I didn't smell good anymore.

ARTHUR   I didn't want to leave.

KELLY   I wish you hadn't. I really wish you hadn't.

ARTHUR   I know, Kelly.

>*Beat.*

>*ARTHUR puts his hand on KELLY's back.*

KELLY   Don't touch me.

ARTHUR   What?

KELLY   DON'T TOUCH ME!

ARTHUR   Okay. I'm sorry.

KELLY   DON'T YOU DARE TOUCH ME!

>*KELLY walks to the desk and starts to take out the books with ARTHUR's letters*

>*He forces it towards ARTHUR.*

>*Beat.*

Read it to me.

Anything.

>*ARTHUR hesitates. . . then complies.*

ARTHUR   "My dear Daniel.

There's a beautiful light creeping through the window this morning and rests upon my face. Last night, as I went to sleep, we lay in the grass together, uncovering hidden images in the clouds. A great chariot racing towards a finish line. A peacock revealing its feathers. Later on we went to the public pool and splashed each other until we fell victim to the chlorine in our eyes. Your butterfly stroke has gotten so strong—you nearly beat me in an epic race that spanned three whole lengths of the pool. We walked home on the paved road near my house, gazing at the crooked trees as they welcomed the fall. You fell asleep on my chest as we watched bad television. You quietly snored, which I thought was so wonderful. I held you as I drifted off to sleep, as the scent of your flowered skin lingered through the sheets.

Thank you for the beautiful poem. Thank you for the wonderful day.

I wait breathlessly until we meet again.

All my love. Arthur."

Beat.

"September, 2001."

KELLY   Are they all like this?

ARTHUR   This is how I learned to cope.

It's a difficult thing to hold on to in here. Faith.

Beat.

KELLY   I was so young.

ARTHUR   And so dear.

KELLY   Dear. I haven't been called that in a while.
              I used to love it when you called me that.

KELLY and
ARTHUR   My dear Daniel.

          Pause.

ARTHUR   Do you ever wonder what things would be like? If I
              wasn't taken away.

KELLY   Every second of every day of my life.

          Beat.

          Do you remember how you would read to me?

          Do you?

ARTHUR   I do.

KELLY   Do you remember when we read *The Once and Future
              King* together?

          Beat.

          I did that, y'know. With Andy? We read that book
          together.

ARTHUR   Kelly, I—

KELLY   Call me Daniel.

>   *KELLY rests his head on ARTHUR's lap.*

>   *KELLY begins to run his head on ARTHUR's crotch.*

>   *Beat.*

ARTHUR   Stop it. Please.

>   *Beat.*

Kelly.

KELLY   Daniel.

>   *ARTHUR gets up.*

>   *Beat.*

What's wrong?

ARTHUR   We can't do that anymore.

KELLY   I want to be close to you.

Don't you love me anymore?

ARTHUR   Kelly—

KELLY   DANIEL. My name is Daniel.

ARTHUR   You should leave.

KELLY   What are you afraid of?

ARTHUR   Don't do this.

KELLY   Don't you want to touch me?

ARTHUR   It's different.

KELLY   I want you to touch me.

I want you to let me touch you. Like before.

ARTHUR   This isn't like before.

KELLY   I'm still me. I'm still the same. I can still write letters.

You love me. Remember? Remember how you love me?

KELLY takes off his shirt.

I have more hair now.

ARTHUR   Put your shirt on.

KELLY   Don't you want to touch my chest?

ARTHUR   Kelly.

KELLY   Daniel.

ARTHUR   You're not Daniel.

67

KELLY   Please, Arthur.

ARTHUR   STOP IT.

KELLY   Don't you like my body?

ARTHUR   I don't want you anymore.

KELLY   Don't say that.

> *KELLY kisses ARTHUR passionately. He tries to unbutton his pants and take off his clothes. ARTHUR pushes him away.*

ARTHUR   I hate it. I despise it.

> *Pause.*

KELLY   You told me you loved me. You told me to have faith in you.

ARTHUR   I do. I did!

KELLY   So why are you doing this? Why are you doing this to me?

ARTHUR   Because it's not... you're not... you're different.

KELLY   Why don't you love me anymore, Arthur? Why won't you touch me?

ARTHUR   You've changed.

KELLY   It's me! It's Daniel!

ARTHUR   You're not. You're not Daniel. You're someone else. You're something else.

KELLY   Why are you doing this? Please, Arthur, don't do this.

ARTHUR   This is not what you want.

KELLY   I need you to love me. I need you touch me.

ARTHUR   Leave. GET OUT!

KELLY   Arthur!

KELLY grasps on to ARTHUR.

ARTHUR   Get away from me. Please. Please, just go.

KELLY   I love you. I love you.

ARTHUR   I can't. I can't. Please go now. Go.

KELLY   ARTHUR!

ARTHUR   GO!

KELLY   ARTHUR!

JOHN comes into the cell. He sees the sight. He rips KELLY from ARTHUR's body.

ARTHUR!

JOHN struggles with KELLY out the door.

ARTHUR!

> *As KELLY is dragged back to his cell we can hear the sounds of him yelling out for ARTHUR.*

> *A very long pause.*

> *ARTHUR goes into his drawer and takes out a pack of matches.*

> *He takes the letters. He lights a match. He lights the letters on fire. He walks to the toilet and stands over it, allowing the letters to burn and ash into the toilet.*

> *JOHN enters.*

> *He watches ARTHUR burning the letters.*

JOHN   What are those?

ARTHUR   These? Nothing. Garbage.

> *Beat.*

> *ARTHUR drops the letters in the toilet.*

All gone.

> *Pause.*

JOHN   I'm leaving.

> *Beat.*

ARTHUR Good.

       Beat.

JOHN I think you should put some thought into…

       I think you've been in here too long.

       Beat.

ARTHUR I think you're right.

JOHN You do?

ARTHUR I do.

       Beat.

JOHN I'm right?

ARTHUR Aren't you?

JOHN Well… yeah, but…

ARTHUR You're confused.

JOHN You think I'm right?

ARTHUR I think…

       I'm…

       Beat.

JOHN   Why do you think I'm right?

         Beat.

ARTHUR   I'd like you to help me, John, to get into programming. I'd like to do the program and I'd like to sit in front of the parole board and I'd like to tell them that I have changed. That I was wrong. That I'd like to leave this place and redefine my life... because this... this is not a life.

         I'd like a life.

         Beat.

         Is that something you can help me with?

JOHN   You don't believe in programming.

         Beat.

         Arthur?

         Beat.

         Do you... think that... that you were wrong... that you're sick?

ARTHUR   I think I need to go swimming.

         Sit in a park. Walk on a beach.

         I'm rotting, John.

I can smell it.

I smell bad.

I'm sick.

I want to get better.

Will you help me?

Beat.

Please.

Pause.

JOHN ...There's some paperwork...

I'll start on the paperwork. Talk to the...

Beat.

How do you know you won't do it again?

ARTHUR Fall in love?

I don't.

JOHN And what if you do?

ARTHUR I don't know.

Beat.

JOHN   Right.

       Beat.

    And that's...

       Beat.

    Right.

       Beat.

    Right.

       Pause. JOHN goes to exit.

ARTHUR   And Kelly?

       Beat.

JOHN   We'll transfer him.

ARTHUR   And then?

JOHN   Try and get him to respond to programming.

ARTHUR   And if he doesn't?

       Beat.

    John?

       Beat.

JOHN   They'll throw away the key.

Pause.

How does that make you feel?

Pause.

ARTHUR   Take care of your family.

JOHN   I will.

ARTHUR   Promise?

JOHN   I pinky swear.

Beat.

ARTHUR   Say hi to your wife.

JOHN   I don't think so.

Beat.

JOHN exits.

Lights.

End of play.

photo by Pierre Gautreau

Michael Rubenfeld is a writer, director, actor and producer originally from Winnipeg, now living in Toronto, Canada. His plays include *Present Tense*, *Spain* and *My Fellow Creatures*.

He is the co-founder and co-artistic director of Absit Omen Theatre with Hannah Moscovitch. In 2008 he was hired as the Artistic Producer of the SummerWorks Theatre Festival.

Michael is a 2001 acting graduate from the National Theatre School.